Practise for Pleasure

A Pocket Guide
for
music students and late starters

by

Pat Legg

First published in Great Britain 1996
by Pit Pat Publishing
28 Patshull Road
London NW5 2JY

A CIP catalogue record for this book is available from the British Library

ISBN 0 9516768 1 4

PIT PAT PUBLISHING

CONTENTS

The Author

Pat Legg was, until recently, teaching cello, and setting up the new Communication and Teaching Skills Courses for the B Mus TCM Degree at Trinity College of Music. She now spends her time writing music (published by Faber Music Ltd) for cellists and teaching Late Starters, as well as accompanying her husband filming butterflies in different parts of the world.

Acknowledgements

The author is grateful to all the students, pupils and teachers who contributed to the survey of what people do in their practising, and how they feel about it; and to

- John Banks and Tessa Addenbrooke for reading through drafts of this book

- Sydna Younson for creating the pictures.

INTRODUCTION

When you are at college you could be spending as much as half your waking hours practising and learning how to play your instrument. It certainly takes up a large part of your life. It would be good if it were, at least *mostly,* enjoyable.

Sadly, this is often not the case.

You probably worry about

- whether you spend enough time practising

- whether you use the time productively or cover the material in the required time

- whether you are ready to take exams or are good enough to give performances.

All of this contributes to a strong sense of under-achievement.

Is it possible to change one's attitudes to practice and use the time more constructively, and so more enjoyably? I believe it is.

HOW TO USE THIS BOOK

This is a book of suggestions. Many of them came from students themselves, - they emerged from a survey carried out in 1993 in three music colleges, gathering students' views about the strengths and weaknesses of their own practising.

Everyone has slightly different needs, and preferences, about practising, so it is up to *you* to select from the ideas set out in the book.

That way you will be able to suit your own particular needs, and also ensure variety: one week you may want to concentrate on memory building, next week on how to get the best out of practising scales, and so on.

You may also find it useful to talk some of the ideas over with your teachers or professors.

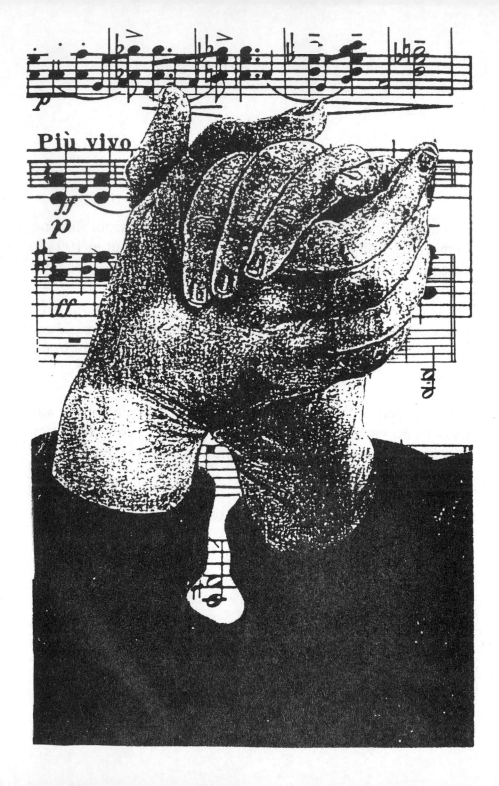

1   THE IMPORTANCE OF PRAISE AND A SENSE OF ACHIEVEMENT

One of the problems about practising is that people spend a lot of time feeling negative about how far they are succeeding in what they have set out to do in their practice sessions. Successful practising depends on keeping in your mind a *balance between awareness of how you have improved and how far you still have to go.* We will get nowhere if we only have a negative perception of our efforts in the activity, and therefore of the activity itself.

So self-praise is essential. Why? Because when one uses negative language it creates negative feelings, and this negative attitude carries through into one's playing. Try turning this around and give yourselves positive feedback. By this I do not mean *gratuitous* praise but rather criticism in the original meaning of the work, - a judgment.

With this kind of thinking, your attitude will be more positive and so will your results.

How to start

Most of us start our practices by playing through something, such as a piece or a study. What is the value of this? It may tell us what is still in need of practice or, if we are lucky, that we do not need to practise that any more. But if we were really going to use our time constructively, wouldn't it have been better either to have begun with some **warm-ups**, or to have gone straight to the **place which you know, from the day before, actually needs to be practised?**

Whatever you choose to do first, it is at this time that you need to ask yourself something positive: "What went well, or at least went better than the last practice?"

If you begin this way, your mind is then more likely to be on a plus rather than a minus, and this will give you a better start to anything else you tackle after that.

It is also a good idea to end your practice on a positive note. If you leave the practice feeling good, you are more likely to want to return to it.

THE "SHAPE" OF A PRACTICE

Let's think some more about how best to "shape" your practice.
It would be helpful to start with something well within your capabilities, them move on to more challenging things and finally return to relatively easy things again. The shape should look something like this:
EASY----------------->>> DIFFICULT ------------------->>> EASY

2

How long should you practise?

In an hour's practice, according to psychologists, the brain takes 10 minutes to get going well, can then concentrate most effectively for 20-40 minutes, and then performs less well for the last 10 minutes. **One-hour practice sessions followed by a break** are probably the most productive, certainly to begin with, though obviously you need to experiment to see what suits *you*.

Try using this diagram to help you see how much time you should spend on each part of your practice:

```
10"<---------------------------30-40"--------------------------->10"
Warm-ups ----- Scales ----- Study -------- Piece for performance
```

Points to remember

☺   The purpose of praise is to build up your confidence. You do this by making positive statements to yourself

☺   Beware of using negative language such as "I can't do this", "It sounds rubbish". This won't help you: in fact, it is more likely to make you feel inadequate

☺   Don't exceed the limit of your own useful practice time

☺   Shape your practice

2   PLANNING YOUR PRACTICE

A schedule

Practice time is valuable. If we wish to use it productively it is probably best to plan it in some way. Also, there are times when we don't wish to practise: maybe we are going through some emotional crisis, or we are just very busy with many commitments, or "we simply can't get down to it". A practice schedule will help you through this kind of difficult time.

It is also important to see your practice time in its proper context: not just as something to be gone through mechanically, but as part of your musical experience, which is developing alongside your technique (see Section 8 on "A philosophy of practice").

You also need to be aware of *over-practising.* If you play for long periods and particularly if you are not using the correct muscles, you can get Repetitive Strain Injury. Planned practice can help prevent this from happening. (For further information on this see Section 6).

Within the practice

How many of us practise or have practised on a day-to-day basis, without really deciding when to do what?

We have seen the value, in Section 1, of following something like the following pattern:

Warm-ups (but do we do them?) **- scales - exercises - studies - pieces.**

Often not enough time is left for the musical side of things: all the time goes on "technique". In fact, "music" can be in all these parts of a practice - see Section 8 again on "A philosophy of practice".

Why do we practise in this order and is it the best use of our time? Would it not help if we had a clear view of our long-term objectives, our short-term aims, and even our daily aims?

We need an overall structure. Not one that is too detailed, but rather one that is flexible and variable.

A well-known musician once said

> *"Routines good or bad are the greatest danger to any player, for they stop the mind from being open and ready for change."*

This of course does not mean you should not do things regularly but rather that you need to **watch out for patterns of behaviour which, repeated mindlessly, do not help you develop your playing.**

Yearly and termly goals

You may find it useful to have a "Year-goal":

> *"By this time next year I will be able to do _____ or at least I will have had a go at ____"*

Remember, your time at college is to develop your playing to the best of your ability. It is the time to investigate and try out things. Where and when will you ever again have such an opportunity to explore, with the consistent help of your professor? Believe it or not, there will, during this time, be fewer outside pressures, such as the need to earn your living, to interfere with your work, than you will ever have later in life.

Having decided on your year-goal, you might like to break it down and think what you could achieve in

   2 x 6-month blocks, or
   3 x 1-term blocks, or
   12 x 1-month blocks.

"By the end of the next six months I would like to feel confident in that part of my instrument that is least familiar to me". Or "this month I would like to improve my tone by considering my embrassure or bow-hold".

7

In these yearly, six-monthly, termly, or monthly plans, keep the aims modest. You are more likely to succeed in them if you haven't set yourself too much, or aimed for something that is well beyond your present abilities.

A weekly plan

For some of us, a *weekly practice outline* can be very helpful.

You can make a mini-contract with yourself, or decide, with your teacher,
- how much time you can give to your practice
- where the emphasis is going to lie in your daily practice
- what proportion of your practice time you are going to spend on each item.

But again the same word of warning; *do not expect too much of yourself.* If you set your goals too high, you won't even get started. But if you can see you are opting out, ask yourself why.

Points to remember

☺   **Planned practices will give you goals to aim for, and help you to feel you are achieving something.**

☺   **Both will add to your overall confidence and help to develop a greater belief in yourself, so that you yourself can control the development of your playing.**

3   DAILY PRACTICE

How much of each day do you spend telling yourself that you must go and practise? Have you ever considered where is the best *place for you to practise, and at what time of day* you are at your best for practising? Students, in answer to our questionnaire, said that they either practised in college or in their bedrooms, and usually during the day, mostly in the mornings.

When?

When is the most productive time to practise? Obviously there is no absolute answer. Some of us work better at one time of day, some at another.

Take the trouble to find out what is your best time.

If we are going into the music profession as performers, then it is important for us to develop the ability to practise and play in the evening as well as during the day - and maybe even in the middle of the night, if we are going to be jet-setting round the world!

Where?

Where should we practise?

Most of us do not have much choice. Where do we ultimately want to play? In a bathroom, bedroom, a tiny studio? No, ultimately we probably wish to be playing in large rooms or halls. They will be of varying sizes. So -

If you possibly can, vary the size of the room you practise in, and always consider the acoustics of that room.

Whenever possible, play in a big space, and with a variety of types of furnishings. Can you play as well in a heavily-furnished room with little reverberation, as you can in a resounding church or hall? Remember, different styles of playing are needed for different types of acoustics, so we need to have experience of playing in a variety of venues.

Thinking about practising

Before we go on to the question of daily practice, let us look at the amount of time we spend on "thinking" about going to practise. Why don't we actually go and do it? What stops us? I think you would be surprised if you counted up the time you spent "thinking" about the need to practise, rather than actually "doing" it. The time could be as much as half an hour. Much better to have practised!

Perhaps the word practising has become highly emotive. Do we set up impossibly high standards for ourselves, ones that we can't hope to achieve and so make the idea of going to practise unattractive?

Maybe practising should not be seen as a chore, but rather as an activity in which we engage in a form of self-development, as well as playing. Try not using the word "practise" but use "play" instead: "I am going to play for a couple of hours".

How much?

Having decided that we want to practise, let us consider the knotty question of how much.

The colleges survey showed that most students practised between 2½ and 3½ hours a day. Yet only a few thought that this was enough. Most of them felt they were not doing enough practise to progress.

Why do we practise?

> **We practise to become better musicians on our instruments with a solid technique so that we can perform confidently.**

But, beware, hours of incorrect playing will only lead to tension, strain and ultimately to despondency about one's progress (see Section 6).

So there are limits to be carefully considered and acted on. We need to build up good muscle control, and good musical awareness. For both of these we need to be able to concentrate, not

11

half-heartedly with our thoughts slipping onto the shopping, going out in the evening etc, but with complete concentration for at least an hour at a time.

It is generally accepted that most people can only concentrate well for about one hour, which is why lectures are usually this length. Then we need a short break. Even in that hour, maybe only 20 minutes is really effective learning.

Three 1-hour practice sessions with breaks are much more likely to be productive than three hours of continuous practice.

Concentration, like muscles, can be developed. If you are someone whose mind keeps wandering during practices, don't worry about it, and especially do not feel guilty. Just notice it is happening. The mind soon learns. Gradually you will find the time between each span of broken concentration will lengthen. Concentration levels can improve in as little as a week.

Why do we lose concentration? In my opinion, it is usually due to boredom or at least because we are not fully engaged in what we are doing. Why is that? Do we think we need to do a certain number of hours just to keep our fingers or embrassure going, and therefore that the mind does not really need to be involved? It is not that simple.

If the mind is not involved in the practice, you are wasting your time. You might as well not be doing it.

In fact there is strong evidence to show that you are more likely to go backwards, if you only practise "on automatic pilot" (see Section 8: "A Philosophy of Practice").

Practise in what order?

What order should you practise things in? Apart from warm-ups, which are intended to do exactly what their name implies, any planned order will do, particularly if it is not the same week in week out.

Depending on what stage you are at, certain things will need more practice than others.

Decide on your own order.

> When I give lessons, - my students get two lessons a week - this is how the contents are arranged.
>
> Studies, scales and improvising in one lesson; and exercises, pieces, transposition, and performance/memorising in the other. Any mixture of these, whatever the student felt comfortable with and had a reason for doing, would have been fine by me.
>
> At the end of each lesson we decide what needs the most practice and the student rearranges his/her practice schedule to suit. It is probably a good idea to keep one order for at least a month, because the regularity helps one to get down to practising and prevents one from flitting from plan to plan.

Do consider improvising, transposition and sight-reading, along

13

with memorising, as part of your daily practice.

Improvising is a useful way of warming up, and gives freedom to your playing. It also increases your harmonic awareness and takes you beyond the constraints of playing only from notation. It can enhance your musical sense in areas such as phrasing and interpretation and can help you cope with a technical problem if you use the problem as an improvising theme.

Transposition (horn players do it all the time!) is an excellent way of developing an understanding of how keys work and to appreciate the tone colour of each key - major, minor and modal. Each group of sounds have different overtones. Start by transposing a simple folk song. You will soon hear the different tone colours of each key.

Sight-reading and memorising are closely linked. If you improve either it will help the other. For any British orchestral player this is a "must". What are the possible problems? Pulse, rhythm, note reading, phrasing and expression. How do you practise them?

The "Super Saver"

There are occasions when we cannot get enough practice time on our instruments. This may be because too much else is going on in our lives, such as too many rehearsals or we are too tired to play or our emotional life is interfering with our routine. This kind of situation can be really stressful particularly if we have a concert coming up.

Why not try a "Super Saver"? It not only helps you through a difficult patch but can also improve the quality of your regular practice.

This is the "Super Saver" I have evolved. You may want to make up your own to suit your needs. Remember to do it when you are feeling good as you certainly won't want to make it up when you need it!

The Super Saver

1   Sit in a comfortable chair (not too spongy) and relax. If you do Alexander Technique, Yoga, Tai Chai or anything similar, then spend a few minutes doing it.

2   In the chair - it can be a in a bus or a train, or wherever you like - take out the music you are working on and imagine you are practising and playing it.

3   Consider the following in relation to the music you are thinking about. Pulse, rhythm, pitch/intonation, expression, phrasing, and tone quality. Also consider the music in relation to any current technical problem. Do all this in your mind.

4   Now, if you still have some time left in your day, practise for 50 minutes, on Warm-ups, and technical problems, and any difficult bits you are about to have to perform.

5   At the end of your 50 minutes. play a piece you know well and really like. This will encourage you if you are feeling down and, because the piece is familiar to you, it will remind your brain and muscles where they should be.

One of the most salutary sayings is

> "If you miss one day's practice, God knows it.
> If you miss two days' practice, you know it.
> If you miss three days' practice, your audience knows it."

Though not strictly correct, it is true that we need, like any other athlete, to keep our muscles in trim, and our brain well coordinated with our muscles. So, Super Savers for emergencies only!

Points to remember

☺   **Spend the time practising rather then thinking about going to practise**

☺   **Discover, when and where is best for you**

☺   **How long can you successfully do concentrated practice?**

☺   **Experiment with venues that have different acoustics**

☺   **Remember to include improvising, transposition, sight-reading and memorising in your daily practice**

☺   **When desperate for time, use the Super-saver.**

Moderato

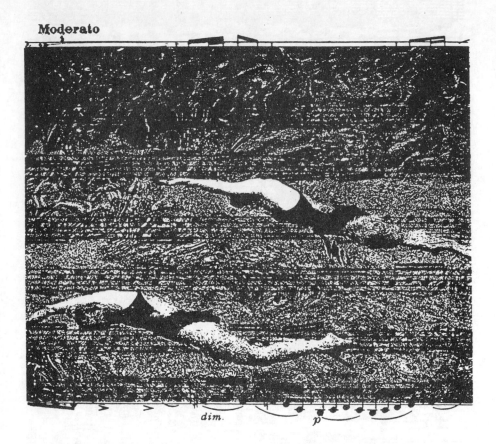

dim.   *p*

4   SCALE PRACTICE

You have probably been struck at some time by the "Chicken and Egg Problem" in relation to playing an instrument.

Which comes first, the good technique or the musicality? Do you need a good technique before you can begin to play musically, or does playing musically show up your weak technical points, which you can then tackle in your practice?

There are some people who believe that unless one practises for hours one cannot get a good technique; and that a great deal of repetitive practice is needed in order to play well. There are others who play mostly music, acquiring the relevant skills as they go along. Maybe the ideal lies somewhere in between, in a balance between the two points of view.

Where do scales etc fit into the pattern of practice? What do they do?

Scales give us an understanding of the precise pattern of sounds in each key, and how they relate to the geography of our instrument. More important, they give us the physical feel of each particular key. If we are familiar with them, they help us to move quickly into different geographical areas of our instrument.

The problem is how do we keep our mind from wandering, -

keeping it, instead, focused on the scale so that it becomes familiar without becoming boring. How many of us think of other things whilst playing our scales etc? Also, most students only get down to practising them seriously when they are about to face an exam.

Here are some suggestions on how to vary your scale practice.

One possible plan is to practise one key a week, which usually means you get through them all in a term.

TERM ONE - A key a week

The aim is to devise a way to cover
    major
    2 minors
    arpeggios
    dominant 7th
    diminished 7th
    chromatic
    any other that your particular instrument requires

- Keep the speed steady so that you have time to think
- Play each note twice ie dd, rr, mm, ff, ss, etc (solfa). This helps you to hear clearly whether each note is in tune. If you are a string-player, listen for the ringing notes ie the sympathetic vibrations with open strings. You can also do this playing each note 3, 4, or even 5 times

- Try singing the note before you play it - in your head if you like. This greatly helps intonation. Research on how the brain works shows that, rather than correct yourself as you go along, you should notice whether you are sharp or flat and then the next time, correct it
- Then, start from the top octave. We are all so used to starting from the bottom that often problems appear only when we start at the top and go down and back to the top. Always go for the unfamiliar, and soon it will be familiar
- Start from the middle, and go down or up and back again
- Play slurred bowings (tonguing for wind), with 2, 3, 4, 5, 6, and 7 notes to a bow (or breath)
- Play with crescendos and diminuendos, and other dynamic variations
- Play at different speeds: it is best to go from slow to fast with the same pulse ie the slow speed halved or quartered to give the fast speeds - rather than getting faster gradually. Then take a new pulse and do the same again. The most important thing is to keep the mind active (see Section 6). Once your mind is no longer concentrating on what you are doing and you are going along on automatic pilot, what you are doing ceases to be of benefit to you. So either change the activity or vary what you are doing. Then you will be making the best use of your time
- Use a variety of different rhythm patterns
- Use a variety of finger action/bowing/tonguing etc such as legato, staccato, etc
- Start and finish on different degrees of the scales eg solfa m

to m, or 3rd degree to 3rd degree, and so on.

TERM TWO - 2 keys a week

Again you have to cover
> major
> 2 minors
> arpeggios
> dominant 7th
> diminished 7th
> chromatic
> any other that your particular instrument requires

- This term, follow the same pattern as Term 1 but set yourself a higher standard and a faster speed.

TERM THREE - Three or four keys a week

- This term, try grouping the keys so as to play consecutively those that have some linking pattern such as similar fingering.
- Write down on slips of paper all the possible combinations for your instrument eg D major separate tonguing 3 octaves, F♯ minor arpeggios slurred 3-to-a-breath from the top, and so on. Put them in a box, so that you can draw them out at random - and play them. This really shows you if you know them.

This yearly schedule can be played over two years if you feel insecure in this area:
- use Term 1 for the first year
- use Terms 2 & 3 for the second year.

Find your own pace, if you can. Sometimes this is not possible because colleges make specific demands. Even within these demands, work out your system of scale practice. Each one of us is different and will need to develop our own routine.

Once you have mastered this yearly pattern, play your scales in some other kind of way. Here are a few suggestions for string players - see what you can devise for piano, wind or brass:

> *What would you do in the middle of a performance if one of your middle strings broke? Would you leave the stage or carry on? If you know your scales and arpeggios using different strings and different fingerings, you could probably carry on...*

- Try playing scales etc on one string only
- Can you play them using
    - first finger only
    - second finger only
    - and so on?
- Try playing them eg G major - first octave only on the G string and starting the second octave on Re on the D string; the third again on Re on the A string; (and the same for the fourth octave on the A, if you are a violinist)
- Try modal scales

- Try whole-tone scales
- Make up your own scales etc

Points to remember

☺   **We practise scales etc to know the geography of our instrument and to play in tune**

☺   **Scales help us to have an understanding of tonality - how different keys sound**

☺   **Always keep the mind active - never play scales automatically**

☺   **Vary the pulse, rhythm, dynamic, direction (ie start at the top, in the middle)**

☺   **Make your own scale practice plan for the term or year or even two years**

☺   **Make up your own scales using different tones and semitones. Also try whole tone and modal scales.**

5   STUDIES AND EXERCISES

Studies

Most of us have been asked to prepare studies, and according to our student survey, most of us dislike the experience. Why?

How often do we just go straight into a study without considering, for instance -

1   Why am I learning this study, and how, at this stage of my development, will it help my playing?
2   Is it a study for the development of the right hand or the left, or both? (Wind: for hands or breath control?)
3   What were the composer's intentions in writing the study?
4   Can I learn the whole study in the time set by my professor?

Probably the most important question to consider is number 4. Many of us professors/teachers happily give students a study a week or even two, saying to ourselves it is similar throughout so the student can easily cover all of it. But the survey showed that most students find more than a study a week overwhelming. Better results come if **students** decide how much of the study they are going to attempt and also for how long they are going to do them.

One possible plan is to do two a fortnight, renewing one a week, ie

    Week 1 - Study A
    Week 2 - Study A and B
    Week 3 - Study B and C
    Week 4 - Study C and D etc

The student gets two lessons on each study. In the first week of a study the preparation is entirely by the student; in the second week the student will have a lesson on it, and in the third week will play it again to the professor/teacher.

If there is a part of the study (eg a couple of bars) where the student would benefit from more repeated practice, then it could go in a "Warm-ups book".

> A "Warm-ups book" is a book made up of any 8-bar sections that are difficult in a study. Add any such difficult passage to the Warm-up Book when you finish the study. Practise 5 of them each day. When you add the 6th, leave number 1 out; when you add the 7th, leave number 2 out, and so on

It may be better for students in their first and second years to get to know their study books, so that later on in their third and fourth and post-grad years, they can choose from the studies which they already know and that will be relevant to their current pieces or technical requirements. In this way students can ask and answer questions 1-4 by themselves (see Section 8 on "A Philosophy of Practice").

26

The question of how much of a study to practise each week or fortnight is a difficult one, and depends very much on the kind of collaboration there is between teacher and pupil (again see Section 8).

How to practise a study

Here are a few suggestions that you may find helpful on how to practise a study.

Beware of just playing it through again after you have had an initial look. Instead, go straight to those parts which you seem to be avoiding because you can't do them. Take them out of context and consider the following:

- Why do I think the problem is here? Could it be before or after I get to this point?

- Often we break down after concentrating and getting over a difficult passage, because in our relief at having succeeded, our concentration lapses. Also sometimes we make mistakes if we tense up in anticipation of something that we think is going to be difficult to play.

- Is the problem to do with
     - reading?
     - hearing - can we hear the intervals in our head?
     - not understanding what the study is for, and reluctance

to ask the teacher in case one seems a fool?
- an inability to play it musically?
- a basic technical problem - one that cannot be solved on one's own?

The problem could also be boredom. The most important aspect of all is to remember that a study is a piece of music that has been composed with a purpose and should be played musically.

Exercises

Exercises need to be considered in the same way as studies: the fundamental challenge is to play them musically. They are often a concentration of physical activity. If you repeat them too often without understanding how to do them or even why you are doing them, you can get Repetitive Strain Injuries. So -

Take great care. Do not tighten up when you are doing exercises

Athletes, instrumentalists, and in fact anyone who uses lot of muscular energy, face a common problem: in playing an instrument we have to have energy/tension in order to push down our fingers or to use our arms; and often other parts of the body are involved - how much depends on the particular instrument. We must also be able to relax once we have used this energy, or else our bodies tense up and we are unable to move freely, which in turn inhibits the sound we are making. The balance between tense

28

and relaxed playing is very fine and we probably spend most of our study time in our first year of studentship trying to achieve this balance.

Here are some suggestions on how to feel this balance:
- Imagine you are in water up to your arms, leaving your arms floating on top of the water, - held up by it but floating at the same time and free to move where they will
- You are a marionette suspended by strings but your weight holds you down
- You are a hot air balloon trying to get off the ground but tied by ropes.

All three metaphors can give you the sensation of balance and weight as well as tension and release in your muscles. Think about them and see if they help your playing.

Points to remember

☺ **Do you know why you have been given a particular study?**

☺ **How much of it can you usefully practise in a week?**

☺ **Difficult passages: put in a "Warm-up" book**

☺ **Would you know where to go in your instrument study repertoire to help you find a particular study that would help** you at the moment you need it?

☺ **Learn to analyse quickly and go straight to the problem in your studies**

☺ **Can you play both studies and exercises musically? Be careful of over-strain**

☺ **As instrumentalists, we need to be perfectly balanced between tension and relaxation.**

6   PRACTICE WITHOUT STRAIN AND INJURY

Are repetitive strain injuries more common than they used to be?

Why is it that athletes, secretaries and computer-users, along with instrumentalists, seem nowadays to be suffering more than ever from Repetitive Strain Injuries - RSI? Is it because they are using their muscles too much, or possibly for too long at a time? Or could it be that they are using them incorrectly?

It is difficult to sort out the answer, but one thing that is clear is that modern methods of training in all four activities have made it possible for humans to do physical activities for far longer periods. Often these activities involve muscles in continuous repetition. For instance, a typist or computer operator no longer has to move his/her hands off the keyboard, even to return the runner; the hands stay in one spot and can continue there for hours on end. Athletes are now expected to train for many hours at a time. Musicians are constantly being told that they must practise at least six hours a day if they are going to make it in the profession.

Understanding RSI and doing something about it

Are we expecting too much of our human frame? Can it adapt to these greater demands, or is it the mental pressures that we impose on ourselves which actually cause the problem? Whatever the answer, you need to take care of your bodies and understand how they work and what they are capable of achieving without causing problems in your playing.

With more and more students suffering from RSI, understanding how we practise takes on a new importance. We need to spend more time considering this. Planning (Section 2) so that we use the time fruitfully and do not misuse or overuse our muscles is one way of preventing the problem arising. Another is thinking about what we are going to practise before we actually do it. This way there will be less repetition of an incorrect kind.

When you are practising, if there is pain, then something is not working properly. You can do something about it. There is no need to live through a pain barrier.

What causes it? The pain is caused by acidic tissue building up around the tendons, or within the muscles themselves, which causes them to become inflamed.

What can we do about it?

We need to understand the kind of things that cause the problem. There have been cases where RSI has been activated by emotional stress. There are many fears and anxieties connected with instrumental playing. We often feel that our future is determined by outside forces over which we have little control. It is important for us to feel that we can control our own lives. Self-reliance and autonomy are a great help in keeping down tension and strain.

Keep fit and well. Take exercise and, above all, as soon as there are any signs of an RSI problem, take it straight to someone who can help you.

Probably one of the best ways of helping yourself is to do "warm-ups" on your instrument before you start playing anything that is physically difficult. No athlete goes straight into a race: likewise no musician should go straight into a heavy practice session. Limber up and make sure your body is not cold.

> *A Finnish friend of mine who had developed tendonitis in both arms, spent two years trying various medical and alternative-medical remedies with little success, and had just about given up the idea of having a music career. Then she visited an old woman in Helsinki who had a reputation for helping people with this sort of problem. This woman noticed that my friend had cold fingertips. she asked her to get her circulation going by always rubbing her fingertips and massaging her wrists and lower arms before she started playing her violin. She did this and within a few weeks the problem had almost entirely gone. A violinist's career was saved by being determined to find an answer.*

By limiting the length of each continuous session, it is possible for us to use our practice time so that it does not contribute to RSI. It has always been said that musicians have to practise long hours in order to build up stamina. This may be true, but the important thing is how you do it.

A good rule is to start with one-hour sessions. Practise for 50 minutes and then take 10 minutes out to give the muscles and tendons - to say nothing of the brain - a rest. As we learn to use our muscles correctly, these sessions can be lengthened. By the end of your first year you will probably find that you can do up to 4 hours a day with no harmful effects.

With new teachers, students are often asked to change many technical things. Try to take one change at a time. If a set of muscles has been used to acting in one particular way, it is going to feel pushed and stretched if asked to go in another direction. The second way may ultimately be better, but remember the tendons and muscles have to move differently and need time to adjust. Take the new ideas slowly. You may well get local pain when you first change but if you change gradually, you will soon not feel the new stretching and so see the benefit. It should only be a minor discomfort. If it is more, then something has not been understood or it is not right for your body. Everyone is slightly physically different so what works for one person may not work for another. Trust yourself to know what is right for you.

It is well worth looking into all the different ways of helping to solve RSI problems. Different things work for different people and to some extent it is the belief in the cure that helps as much as the cure itself. There is no single way to help RSI. The Alexander Technique has helped many people: so has Yoga, Tai-Chai, Faith-healing, Hypnosis, and Acupuncture, as well as physiotherapy, osteopathy, and other medical treatments.

One further point for you to consider: does emotional stress for some players become so great that they have to find an excuse to stop playing? This is not to say that the problem is not real but rather that it has been brought on by a deep-rooted desire not to play, and this "not wanting to play" causes RSI so that the player has to give up.

Points to remember

☺   **Don't forget you can avoid getting RSI by doing a good bit of your practice away from your instrument - see the Super-Saver**

☺   **Never start from cold, and always stop if there is a continuous physical problem; get help as soon as possible**

☺   **Look into different ways of avoiding/solving the problem of tendonitis and find the solution that suits you.**

7   MEMORY-BUILDING AND SIGHT-READING

How to practise memory-building

Memory-building, like any other skill, requires practising if it is to be developed.

How do people memorise?

The normal process is what is known to psychologists as "proceduralisation". Many musicians learn their music by proceduralisation. This means that they memorise the music so that a whole phrase will follow an initial trigger. This frees their attention to concentrate on other aspects of playing such as interpretation, following a conductor, or listening to others in the ensemble. Proceduralisation can fail us; it is not 100% reliable, and often the cause of failure is stress.

What kinds of memorising are there? There are two:

> - short-term memory, to remember things like telephone numbers ie a number sequence, or a phrase like "To be or not to be..."

> - long-term memory, for storing and retrieving information.

As musicians we use both, and we need a successful system of recall.

In what ways do musicians memorise? By sight, sound, and touch. The three help each other. We use

> ***symbols:*** ie the printed music. We see visually what is on the page. The shapes help us to recall the page. Some people have photographic memory but it can be a disadvantage as it does not allow you to "proceduralise".

> ***sound:*** We hear the musical logic of a line. If we can sing it accurately then we will play it accurately as well. But in fast passages, and where there are rests, this can let us down and again not allow us to "proceduralise".

> ***touch:*** We have the physical feeling of the hand as we play the instrument, but again this is not always reliable.

Often different surroundings can upset the memory, particularly if you have always practised in the same room. So can wearing different clothes ie ones especially for a concert.

How can we help ourselves to be sure that our memory will not fail us?

To understand the music thoroughly, and to consider it in different ways so that all approaches are covered. If the visual fails, then aural and touch will take over.

We all memorise in different ways in a combination of the above. It is important to find your own way.

Wherever you falter in your practice is where your memory will fail unless you check it out and find out why. Sort it out while there is plenty of time. Doing it near the performance time leads to anxiety.

Here are some suggestions that may help you:

- When sight-reading, try to be accurate straight off. If you make a mistake at this stage it can often be difficult to eradicate later. If you get the chance, look at the music before you play it and see where you think the traps are. See if you can look at the bar ahead while you are playing the bar behind

- If you have a rhythmic problem, consider the rhythm only. Often the rhythm is in the stem of the notes:

Example:

Tap the rhythm out on your knee so that you feel it as well as see it. Tap the pulse with one hand while you tap the rhythm with the other. Swop hands (you will find the exercise difficult but if you can do it away from the instrument you will have no problem when you play it).

Dalcroze Eurhythmics very much involves the development of the physical and mental approach to rhythmic patterns and pulse. I suggest you dip into "Dalcroze Today" by Marie Buchanan.

Also, try improvising a melody using the rhythm which presents a problem. (You can also do this with interval problems.)

- Interval problems and pitch. Try singing tricky bits in your head. If you know solfa, see if you can sing it that way, then sing it to interval names ie major 3rd, minor 6th etc, also tones, semitones etc, - and finally to letter names. Each way reinforces the memory process so by the time you have done it the 4 ways (inner hearing; solfa; intervals; and letter names) you will really have learnt it.

- How music is written on a page can also be a problem. Music ought to be written out with all bars and notes spaced equally, in such a way as to represent the time passing regularly. But whereas it should look like this -

a)   ♪♪♪ ♪♪♪ | l ♪ l ♪ | ♪♪♪ l ♪ | l· l· | (Equal spacing)

often it looks more like this -

b)   ♪♪♪   ♪♪♪ |l·l·|♪♪♪ ♪♪♪| l· l· | (Unequal spacing)

40

The condensation of the notation in b) of course makes it cheaper for the publisher; but it often causes reading problems and therefore memorising difficulties. A way to get round this is to enlarge the music on a photocopier (I believe the publishers do not mind if it is a part of a work for your own use, so long as you have already bought the music and destroy the photocopy once you no longer need it).

Having tried all the above methods you may find you still have problems sight-reading and memorising. Maybe what you really have is some kind of emotional block. These suggestions might be of some help:

- allow yourself to be wrong - after all, this time is not the performance, - and in letting go you may well find you can do it

- only gradually put yourself in situations where you need to rely on your memory - if possible non-threatening situations - and again remind yourself that it is a learning experience and you can allow yourself to go wrong

- don't worry about what anyone else thinks. It is not their problem. You are going to solve it for yourself

There are medical ways of helping you to relax so as to give yourself every chance to be unstressed, but they can affect your memory so be careful (see Section 10 on Stress in Performance).

Probably the most important of all is the point we keep returning to - that you yourself believe that you can memorise, if not now, then in the very near future.

Points to remember

☺ Sight-reading and memorising are linked

☺ Use the two kinds of memory-building - short-term and long-term

☺ We learn to memorise by sight, sound and touch

☺ We need to test our memory in different settings

☺ Where we falter in practice is where we fail in memory

☺ When sight-reading, separate rhythm and pitch

☺ Give yourself permission to be wrong when trying out your memory. This way you will not mentally block because of emotional tension

8   A PHILOSOPHY OF PRACTICE

As we said earlier in this booklet, we practise so that we can play and our ultimate aim is to play well. To do this we need

- a good technique

- a well-developed musical appreciation and understanding

- a strong belief in ourselves.

The three go together and all need to be practised together. They are like the three sides of a triangle and are interdependent.

How often have we heard someone playing who has a wonderful technique but has left us feeling cold and empty? They seem only to be technicians.

How often have we heard a musical and potentially very beautiful performance marred by an inadequate technique?

As a teacher this kind of situation leaves me particularly sad. Somewhere one of us have failed to give this pupil a thorough understanding of how their instrument works.

Again how often have we heard a performance that would have

been enjoyable had the performer not conveyed a feeling of self-doubt, which left the audience feeling insecure and uncomfortable?

It would be as well to keep these three concerns in mind whenever we are practising.

Technique

What are the possible pitfalls that lead to the first kind - the *over-*technical approach?

- repetitious practice that only considers the physical actions, with just the fingers working but the mind not engaged
- repetitious practice that doesn't involve questioning what you are doing. You may need to ask yourself "Why can't I do it?-
  - is it psychological?
  - is it technical?
  - do I understand the process of this technical point?
  - do I know how to put it right?
  - what is the composer trying to say?"

Practice which never queries why or how a particular thing is being practised is often the result of being told too precisely what to do. The student has no responsibility for the process. I'm sure you would agree that there is no point repeating something unless you fully understand how to do it and what it is for.

46

Musicianship

How can we develop our musical sense while we are practising? One way is by considering the following musicianship qualities and integrating them into our technical practice:

pulse: many students find they have a poor inner pulse. This can be considered and corrected in scales, exercises and studies. While playing, feel not only the pulse of the music but the pulse that goes twice as fast. This stops the music from being hurried

rhythmic awareness: changing from one kind of rhythmic pattern to another within a self-given pulse. Don't forget to include rests in the Exercise, and also keep changing the speed of the pulse. Try giving yourself speed indications such as Largo, Andante, con fuoco, Allegro etc. This can be practised in scales, exercises and studies

pulse and rhythm can provide drama in music:

- playing the music faster can add a sense of urgency and lead the music forward
- delaying the tempo fractionally can give a nostalgic feel to the music
- playing the music strictly in time makes it feel that it is being played in the here and now

quality of sound: if the tone quality is poor we can often learn from the sound what is technically amiss. Listen to your instrument. It will tell you by the sound when it is not happy!

expression: mood, dynamic range and style (in the baroque, for example) can all be practised on scales, exercises and studies

types of articulation: as one very good teacher said: "There can be as many types of articulation as there are consonants in the alphabet". Varying articulation gives colour to our tone quality

form: an awareness of harmonic and melodic structure. Look for it in studies and make up your own in scales and exercises by improvising

phrasing: to my mind this is the most important thing in the development of musical awareness. Phrasing is really the way we talk musically. Phrases state, search, answer, or reflect; and are lyrical, tragic, humorous etc. We understand best those players who phrase the most eloquently. Phrasing is also a sense of timing.

Self-confidence

All too often we believe that other people have all the answers. But time at college should be spent in developing our ability to be self-critical and in learning the process of how to teach ourselves to become a professional musician.

The professor's/teacher's aim should be make him/herself redundant as soon as possible; the pupil's aim, to control, and be responsible for, their own musical growth as soon as possible.

Perhaps it looks something like this:

Knowledge to pass on

Arrive at college

TEACHER

PUPIL

Leave college

<-->
1st, 2nd, 3rd, 4th year (of a 4-year course)

Knowledge to receive

If you do not understand something your teacher is telling you or showing you, there is everything to be gained from asking for an explanation.

Teaching is a two-way process - an exchange of ideas. I have both learnt and cleared my own thoughts about many aspects of playing by students asking or querying things I have suggested to them.

Remember everyone is different and there are many successful ways of doing things and many right answers, not just one.

Points to remember

☺ **We need equally**
- **a good technique**
- **good musical understanding and appreciation**
- **a strong belief in our own capability**

☺ **To achieve these three, we need to**
- **ask questions**
- **avoid mindless repetition**
- **develop our musical awareness hand-in-hand with our developing technique**
- **believe in ourselves, knowing that what we have to offer, however little in the early stages, is important to the process of becoming a professional musician.**

9   PREPARING FOR EXAMS

Even though many of us like giving performances, very few of us like taking exams. But since exams are part of the preparation needed to enter the profession, we need to try to improve our attitude to taking them.

Basically we are afraid of them, but what is it that we are afraid of? The unknown, - we do not know what is expected of us. So the first step is to get to know the syllabus. Confront the requirements early on: start now. Find out what is expected of you in your next exam.

The language of the syllabus often seems difficult and threatening. So we need to sidestep the language, by writing down in clear and simple words what it is that we will be doing. It can then be mulled over and so prepared for in advance.

You should then find out what percentage of marks is given for each part, and work out why. Find out which are the areas in which you feel least comfortable or competent. Most things, including sight-reading (see Section 7), can be prepared in advance. One way of taking exams successfully is to think of them as very detailed performances with all your preparation on display as well as your playing. Imagine the programme has been chosen for you by your agent and that you will have to talk about it.

sempre dim. al fine

Helping ourselves in advance

You must know really well all aspects of the works you are going to have to play or write about.

- for written papers, you can have a card system for memorising. Write the key points on one side and the explanations for the key points on the other. See if you can remember the explanations by only looking at the key points

- for scales etc, keep your brain stimulated and awake (see Sections 4 on Practising Scales and Section 6 on A Philosophy of Practice)

- mental preparation: fear causes panic, so you need to go into the exam feeling you have done all that you could possibly have done at this time. Find ways of coping with exam pressure. Keep away from others taking the exam: fear is easily passed on, particularly before an exam. Do not go in for post-mortems after the exam. It's too late and does you no good

- plan your use of time leading up to the exams. There seems so much to do. Where do you begin? Make a plan of the term before the exam (usually in the summer) so that you know what commitments you have and what time you have for preparing.

Your health

Some people can get a lot of help from Yoga, Tai Chi, the Alexander Technique, transcendental meditation, and other things: you should know what they offer, and see what they can or cannot do for you.

Diet: eat well, following a balanced and healthy diet. This is difficult on a grant, but you should not economise on fruit and vegetables whatever else you do. You need the energy which food gives you. Why not take all the help you can get?

Exercise: take some form of exercise at least every other day. Sporty or not, musicians have to use their bodies in much the same way as an athlete, and need to take similarly good care of them. Warm-ups, gym, walks, swimming - all can help you avoid stress and other physical problems - even cycling to college helps. Have your plan, and stick to it.

Feel good about yourself: make sure you give yourself enough positive encouragement and praise - see Section 1.

When preparing for exams give yourself a day off - say a Saturday evening to Sunday evening, perhaps practising on Saturday morning and Sunday evening. Enjoy this time off: do something completely different. It will help to clear your mind.

Divide your day into concentration periods. Here is an example - though your choice may well be different

- Practise 1 hour, then take a ¼-hour break. Then do a different activity connected with the exam

- Practise for another 1 hour then take another ¼-hour break. Then do a different activity connected with the exam

- Repeat the sequence...and so on, and stop for lunch!

At the end of each week, if you have completed your plan, then give yourself a pat on the back. If you have not completed it, no matter for what reason, do not feel guilty. Guilt will not help you: in fact it may even stop you from practising the next day. Just start afresh the next day and put your plan into action.

> *A niece of mine did little work until the last 5 weeks of term, and then made a plan and kept to it. She got quite a good result. The next year, using the same system, she started working seriously earlier, and did very well.*

Many musicians are not very used to using words. Make a point of discussing things about your music with friends, especially teaching topics. When answering a question at a viva, use a firm voice, and don't rush yourself. If you don't understand the question, say "If you mean so and so..., then the answer could be...", or "Do you mean...?".

Points to remember

☺ **Look at the syllabus in plenty of time, and pick out the main requirements. Concentrate on the areas you know least well**

☺ **Prepare in advance: put written work on key cards; prepare yourself mentally; timetable your practice**

☺   **Keep healthy; diet, exercise yourself, and take a day off**

☺   **Readjust your timetable at the end of each week**

☺   **Make a habit of talking about your work.**

An exam check list

Pieces
Scales*
Sight-reading*
Memory-building*
Aural tests
Improvising
    rhythm work
    singing in your head
The viva voce exam

*see Section 4

57

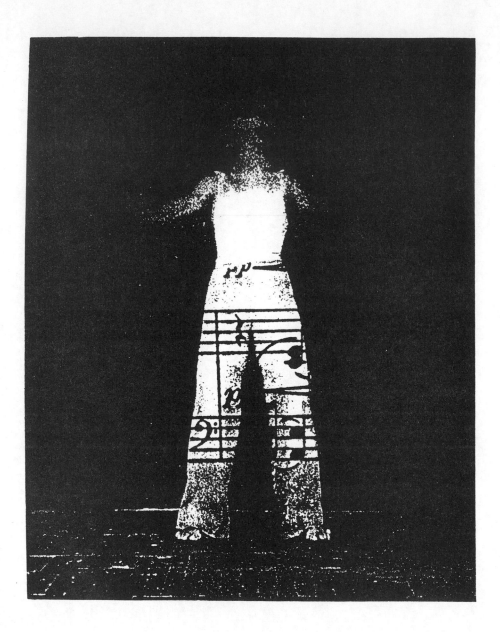

10   STRESS IN PERFORMANCE

Going out on to a stage or platform can be gruelling experience. We often frighten ourselves by saying something like this:

> *I have to go out on to that stage and give a perfect performance. I only have one chance. I shall fail in the profession if I do not get it right and nobody will ever ask me to play again.*

How many of us have terrified ourselves with this kind of remark? They are of course no possible help or use to us. We can even be anxious when we play to someone we admire or wish to impress.

We would of course much prefer to go out on the stage and convey our love of the music to the audience. Why do we put ourselves under such stress, and how can we help ourselves to have only a positive attitude to performance?

What is our ultimate aim?

To give an enjoyable performance and show through our playing how we see the music. (We can even influence our audience's response to it).

What are the signs of stress?

Usually, sweaty palms, uncontrollable shaky muscles, tension, shortness of breath or racing breathing, un-focused eyes, dry mouth, dizziness, tingling fingers, head-ache at the back of the head and neck.

What situations put us under stress?

Playing to one's peer group. Playing to one's professors. Playing when the performance is important to one's career, as in auditions.

What are we afraid of?

Memory lapses? Undermining inner voices? Lack of self-confidence? Criticism?

Fear of criticism can be one of the worst causes of stress. But criticism can imply good or constructive criticism as well as bad or destructive.

> *We should remember this when someone else is giving a performance. Do we only offer negative criticism? Remember it will be your turn next. How much better it is if we first praise someone's playing by saying something positive such as "It was musical. The bowing technique was good, - and so on". You could ask yourself what the performance could teach you? You would probably appreciate it if someone was*

asking this about your performance instead of only being negatively critical.

How can we cope with stress?

The best way is through autonomy, a healthy belief in yourself and your abilities.

How do we achieve that?

- *build up your concentration:* notice in practice and performance how much the mind wanders.

Have specific targets such as feeling the pulse/rhythm, listening to the tone/intonation/phrasing to get your concentration back. Be aware of the musical structures of the piece, and see how quickly you can memorise what you are playing. This all helps to keep your mind from wandering and so to avoid stressful thoughts.

- *build up your aural awareness:* keep an internal pulse and notice the rhythm over the top. Sing in your mind as you play. Internal hearing builds up an understanding of the music which gives confidence in performance.

- *decide on and carry out your practice plan:* how much practice do you need to give you security? (see Section 2). Really believe in your plan, and then when you go out on stage, really believe in what you have done.

61

Medical help?

There are drugs you can take which can help you but try them out before the actual performance because some have a much stronger effect on some people. Some performers use Beta Blockers. Herbal drugs can also be helpful.

Deflection

A good book to read on this approach is "The Inner Game of Music" by Barry Green and W Timothy Gallwey.

Alternatives to medical help

As I have mentioned before, many people with problems of stress have found the following helpful: Tai Chi; Yoga; Transcendental Meditation; hypnosis; the Alexander Technique.

Everybody is slightly different and what can work for one person may not for another. Go on trying out all possible ways until you find what works best for you.

Psychological barriers

Stress problems are often not so much physical as psychological. Don't let your playing become the be-all and end-all of your life. There must be other things in it too. The important thing is to know yourself. Try to develop your whole person. Follow up other interests besides your playing.

There are of course some people who need to be under stress while they perform. Or at least it is only under stress that they perform at their best. But beware: for most of us the wear and tear on the nerves will surely lead to some sort of crack-up. We all need a certain amount of adrenalin in our veins to assist our performance but too much will lead to short breaths, and woolly fingers and limbs.

Dr Martin Elliott has done a great deal of research on the psychological aspects of performance and the "tyranny" of the instruments we play. If you have a chance to hear him talk on the subject, I recommend you do so.

Some final tips to think about while you are playing...

☺   Release of tension: start by giving yourself *permission to be wrong*. This frees the mind to concentrate on specific aspects that will assist you to play.

☺   Consider your *physical balance*. How are your feet? Are you distributing your weight comfortably on them? Where is the centre of your physical balance? Again it takes the mind off focussing on failure.

☺   How is your *jaw*? Is it clenched? Thumbs are connected to the jaw, so check them for tension. This also frees the mind from

63

anxiety.

☺ Is your *neck* free? THINK (not do) about your shoulders opening out and particularly that your armpits are open. Feel your arms balanced like a mother hen embracing her chickens, or feel that a couple of helium balloons are holding up your arms.

☺ Imagine your ***elbows and fingertips*** are moving out in opposite directions. This frees the tendons and allows you to move your arms more freely.

☺ How about

- your ***breathing***? "Think" of your breath coming out of all your body. It helps to get rid of excessive adrenalin

- your ***surrounding body***? Imagine you are enclosed by a line running around the outline of your body. It helps you to feel safe and it will help you to breathy normally and focus properly.

If you give a bad performance don't go into a decline but talk it over with someone you trust and who really wants to help you. Take it as a way into understanding how you can improve this aspect of your playing so that it is less likely to happen again. I stress the word "less" as these kinds of problems rarely immediately disappear. You have to work on them and then suddenly you realise they are no longer with you. And remember

64

we have all had them!

☺ Avoid your inner voice giving you negative feedback. Divert your mind by thinking about specific aims

☺ When you listen to a colleague's performance, start by reflecting on the good points. It will help you when you are giving your own performance

☺ Stress problems are most often psychological. To help with them, don't neglect all the other aspects of your life

☺ Think of a "bad" performance as something to be learnt from. Don't castigate yourself but ask why did it happen? Was it
    - technique?
    - musicianship?
    - lack of preparation?
    - fear of others (lack of self-respect)?
    - fear of failure (setting yourself too high a standard for the stage you are at)?

☺ Our worst enemy is the CD recording. We hear only perfect performances, ones that we cannot possibly reproduce. Remember that they are rarely truly live performances but ones that have been made perfect in the recording studio, which you cannot possibly reproduce in the concert hall.

11 PREPARING FOR PERFORMANCE

Performing lies at the heart of playing any instrument. Why do we play at all, except to give ourselves and others joy from the music? Performing is the link between the composer and the audience provided by the player.

As the poet Rilke says, "Enjoy the moment". Really live the experience.

Easier said than done? To start with, here are some general dos and don'ts to keep in mind.

- Play within your capabilities: the audience should not be embarrassed by a player's lack of skill - though this is a matter of degree: musical feeling can make up for some technical deficiency particularly in early performances

- Start by playing to friendly audiences who you know will give you constructive feedback

- When you are the audience, let your criticism be friendly; remember that you will be next...

Performing implies acting in front of people. You are there to give: so you need to think out what is it that you have to give - that you want to share with the audience. As musicians, we spend a lot of time punishing ourselves, criticising our level of attainment, and so on: when performance time arrives we have to turn into extrovert persons who have a message and are confident about giving it out to others.

We have different "voices" in which we do it:

- the orchestral voice
- the chamber voice
- the solo voice.

We need to adjust to perform well in each. An inappropriate voice will be felt by the audience.

Preparation

There is plenty we should do to prepare for performance. Let's think about it in two main parts: the external and physical context: and the internal, - personal and psychological.

The externals

We need to be clear about where the performance is to take place, because the site and nature of the venue will affect how you project the performance:

- how much rehearsal time is there to be in the hall or elsewhere nearby? Is it enough?

- how are the acoustics? ringing or dead? how will they differ when there is an audience present?
- are stands provided and are they firm? how are the players' chairs to be set out and are they comfortable, and who is responsible for ensuring that your chair/seat is how you want it?
- are there to be flowers to decorate the hall?
- who is going to turn the pages for you?
- how is your spike to be located? are all your reeds OK? do you have spare strings? don't forget your mute
- are there lighting arrangements and who is going to put them on or bring them up?
- is the heating OK? is the stage draughty?
- how are you to dress? formal or informal? Be careful what you wear: many musicians wear clothes that are far too fussy and detract from the listening process.

Now how about *the audience*? Is the programme well-suited to their interest? You need to have a relationship with them so the order and selection should be arranged with them in mind.

Programmes can be arranged in many ways but here are some ideas to start you thinking:
- the most usual sequence for items is to put the older first and to go on to the more modern
- you can try it another way: old to new to old
- you can have all the items from one era
- if any item is unaccompanied, will it be better for all the

programme to be so?
- a "fun" piece may go well at the end, to send the audience
away happy, particularly as an "encore". Alternatively,
a quiet piece has a calming effect.

How about *programme notes*? You could cover the origins of the
pieces (when they were first played or found): offer some thoughts
about the best or best-known parts; and particularly historic
performances. If you feel up to it, much can be added to the
audience's enjoyment if you SAY something about the piece
before you play it. It does not have to be a lot: but rehearse it
beforehand aloud and do not go on too long.

Think about how you are going to get on and off the stage. On the
stage, you need to be comfortable, and it is important to foresee
and deal with any difficulties of a practical kind. Your projection
of yourself on stage, and the audience focussing on you, are all
part of your performance. They affect the degree of comfort and
enjoyment you can generate in your audience. Be sure to
acknowledge the audience's applause properly - however modest
the performance has been.

The internals

This is about you. You are going to take your audience on a
journey through music. You may like to put a piece at the
beginning which gives you confidence and establishes a
comfortable feeling of rapport between you and your audience.

Can you sense them listening to you? If not, why not?

You need to be able and ready to live a bit dangerously if you are going to perform well. This means you have to have confidence and the important way to achieve that is to prepare well and have the right attitude of mind. So how do you go about that?

Practice

You must do enough practice to build up and ensure your feeling of security. Once you are out there, really believe in what you have done. Prepare at least a couple of months ahead.

Put your pieces to bed when you have done a lot of work on them. They will go on mulling themselves over in your brain without your practising them again. Then get them out and revise and rememorise them (see Section 7 on Memory Building).

Choose your time of day for practising if you can. Find out why it suits you best. Try playing and practising at the time you are going to perform. Eating a big meal before you play will cause the blood to go to your stomach and away from your brain. But don't go hungry onto the platform.

In the end you can only practise within the practicable limits of the time available to you. Do not feel guilty that you cannot do more than that!

Be kind to yourself. Do not be negative about your achievement. Value yourself (see also Section 8 on "A Philosophy of Practice").

Performance

Some practical tips to help you keep relaxed and concentrated when on the stage:

- go through your warm-ups before you go on the stage

- imagine the space between your fingers, which releases the tension in both hands

- take extra care to ensure you are sitting or standing comfortably

- tune the instrument before you go on the platform, but check the tuning on the platform: take your time, and don't feel rushed. Be sure you are adept at tuning in front of other people. This needs practice. It is one of the hardest things we have to do

- think along with your pieces as you play them: does the audience understand what you are trying to tell them? Remember you are the one in charge; the audience does not know the music as well as you do

- act the part: give the performance, see yourself as an actor whom the audience must enjoy watching as well as listening to

• too much adrenalin? you can get rid of the sensation by thinking it out through your feet, your fingers, and the top of your head

• strategies for controlling stress: remember
    - keep the inner pulse going
    - think about what you are intending to project
    - relax the neck; back; thighs; upper arms; armpits; jaw; and thumbs. And feel the ground under your feet.

Conclusion

Music is the only language that is world-wide. We are lucky to be able to be use it to communicate with others. Many people in many countries just sit down and play their instruments with, and to, other people without anxiety, only with pleasure. To some extent we have lost this ability. It would be very good if we could all take our instruments out of their cases and happily play to anyone at any time, just for the sheer joy of it.

To be able actually to enjoy practising is a step towards to this end.